Who were Martha and Jonathan Kent and Eben and Sarah Kent?

Why was the early Superman less powerful than today's Man of Steel?

Who was the <u>first</u> movie Superman?

Why did crew members throw birds at Christopher Reeve while the cameras were rolling?

How did Darth Vader change Superman's life?

You'll find the answers to all of these questions—and much, much more—inside this special collectors' book of inside info and movie memories, which we call . . .

Original design by Joe Orlando and Michael Fleisher. This abridged version by Alix Serniak and Jovial Bob Stine. New text by Jovial Bob Stine. *Superman III* text by Chip Lovitt.

ISBN 0-590-32950-2

This edition is published by Scholastic Inc., 730 Broadway, New York, NY 10003, by arrangement with DC Comics Inc.

12 11 10 9 8 7 6 5 4 3 2 1   9   3 4 5 6/8

Printed in the U.S.A.

The Great SUPERMAN™ Movie Book!

Confidential Close-Ups, Fantastic Facts, & A Fabulous Photo Collection

SCHOLASTIC INC.
New York Toronto London Auckland Sydney Tokyo

CONFIDENTIAL CLOSE-UP:
Meet CHRISTOPHER REEVE

"**W**hen I became an actor, my family was really surprised," says Christopher Reeve. "My parents are very serious people. When I was a kid, we didn't even have a TV set!"

Chris was born in New York City on September 25, 1952. His father is a professor and writer. His mother is a newspaper reporter.

"My parents didn't think TV was good for us," Chris says. "So my brother and I had to make up our own entertainment. We used to play in empty cardboard cartons. We pretended they were pirate ships. We used our imaginations. I think that's what got me hooked on acting."

Chris's parents got divorced. Chris's mother married again, and the family moved to New Jersey.

"My stepfather had four children," says Chris. "That made

six kids in the house, counting my brother and me. The house was really crowded. I think acting and dreaming about the theater became my escape."

When he was 15, Chris got a job helping out at a summer theater. He went to high school while he worked at the theater. The theater began taking up more and more of his time.

"I loved that theater so much," Chris says. "But I began to feel guilty. I thought I wasn't giving enough time to school. So I joined as many school clubs and teams as I could. I played on the ice hockey team. I was in the school orchestra. I even sang with a choral group!

"But more and more, I felt that the theater was my home. It was what I did best."

NOT A NEWCOMER

Several years later, Chris was picked to play Superman and Clark Kent in the movies. A lot of newspapers said he was a newcomer. But he wasn't.

He had already starred in a play with actress Katharine Hepburn. And he had been on daytime TV for two years. He was on the soap opera *Love of Life*.

"I played a very evil person," says Chris. "But the viewers loved him."

Well . . . not *all* of the viewers. One day Chris was sitting in a restaurant. A woman came up and whacked him over the head with her purse. "How *dare* you treat your poor wife that way!" she shouted. She was mixing

Chris up with the character he played.

"I was on that soap opera for two years," says Chris. "I didn't want to be on that long. I wanted to do other acting jobs. But I wanted to earn enough money to pay back my step-father for putting me through college."

Now that he is a big star, Chris doesn't have to worry about money. But he worries about something else.

"I don't want to be known just as Superman," he explains. "I want to be known as an actor who can do all kinds of things."

So, Chris has done all kinds of things in recent years. He starred in such movies as *Somewhere in Time* and *Death Trap*. And he appeared in a Broadway play called *Fifth of July*.

A DARING RESCUE

But what does Christopher Reeve enjoy playing most? You guessed it—Superman!

"When I get in that costume, something takes over," he says.

"One time, Lois and Superman were supposed to be flying over Metropolis. Margot Kidder and I were hanging from a rig 30 feet above the studio floor.

"Suddenly the rig began to crack. Margot screamed: 'Somebody get us out of here!'

"I felt so much like Superman that I actually reached out my hand to catch her!"

Chris says he tried to play Superman the way most people think of him. "I was brought up on Superman," he says. "Everyone knows how he stands—hands on hips, cape blowing in the breeze. That's the way six and a half billion people have loved Superman, and I wouldn't dream of changing it.

"Superman is fun to play," Chris says. "But Clark Kent is a lot more fun. That's because he's such an awful mess!"

Chris breaks out in a laugh. It's easy to see that he's having a great time bringing the fun of Superman to millions of movie fans.

CONFIDENTIAL CLOSE-UP:

Meet MARGOT KIDDER

"**I**'m a lot like Lois Lane," says Margot Kidder. "She has lots of energy, and so do I. She is a newspaper reporter, and that's what I wanted to be. In fact, I worked on a newspaper for a while. I found that I was just as sneaky as Lois. I was always trying to get people to tell me their darkest secrets."

It's no dark secret that Margot also dreamed about being an actress.

"When I was a kid, we lived in tiny mining towns in Quebec, Canada," Margot says. "I used to read every movie magazine I could get my hands on. I had to sneak them into the house. My parents thought they were trashy.

"I used to read them and daydream. Sometimes I'd pretend to be a princess. Other times I imagined I was a movie star."

ters. When she was 16, her family settled in Vancouver.

DREAMS START TO COME TRUE

Margot got a job at a local TV station. She began to take any kind of acting job she could get. "I didn't really know what I was doing," Margot admits. "I just knew that I wanted to act!"

She was still only 16 when a Hollywood director saw her. He asked her to try out for a new film called *Gaily, Gaily*.

Margot paid her own way to Hollywood. "I would have walked there to take that screen test!" she says. She got the part! She's been making movies ever since.

NOT THE STAR TYPE?

"Lois Lane is a dream role," Margot says. "People keep telling me that the role will make

Margot's dream came true. Playing Lois Lane has made her a star.

She started out in a small town called Yellow Knife in Canada. That's where she was born. Her early years were spent traveling from one town to another. She had four brothers and sisme a star. I think that's silly. I'm just not the star type. I'm not mysterious, and I'm not glamorous."

A lot of people would disagree with that—including Superman!

How did Margot feel about flying with Superman? How did she feel about the dangerous flying scenes?

"They were fairly easy," she says. "The long flying scenes were a problem. I'd get very tired during them. They seemed to take forever.

"But after all the hours of hanging over the studio floor, I finally saw the flying scenes on film. Then I knew it was all worth it. I was amazed at how real it looked! And I was amazed at how beautiful it was. I was really impressed!"

Margot must have been *really* impressed with the flying scenes. When she finished filming *Superman II*, she took up a new hobby—hang gliding!

CONFIDENTIAL CLOSE-UP:

Meet THE VILLAINS

Terence Stamp: GENERAL ZOD

"Today's villains are too human," says actor Terence Stamp. "The bad guys in movies today always have some nice qualities, too."

That's *not* the case with the character Stamp plays in *Superman II*—General Zod. "Zod is brutal, evil, and corrupt," says Stamp.

Stamp was born in England in 1939. His father was a tugboat captain. Stamp quit school when he was 15. By the time he was 20, he had become an actor.

He has made dozens of films in the United States and in Europe. Maybe you've seen him on TV in such movies as *Billy Budd* or *The Mind of Mr. Soames*.

"Playing General Zod was very refreshing," he says. "It was a refreshing change to play someone who can be described in one word—*evil!*"

Sarah Douglas, URSA

Sarah Douglas found that her role as Ursa was a nice change, too. "I was in movies like *The Land That Time Forgot*," she says. "I always played the lovable girl who gets rescued just in the nick of time.

"Ursa was a real change for me. Especially since I'm not like her at all. I'm really rather romantic. I like ruffles and lace."

How did Sarah prepare herself to play such a mean person?

"Mostly, I just thought nasty thoughts," she says.

Jack O'Halloran: NON

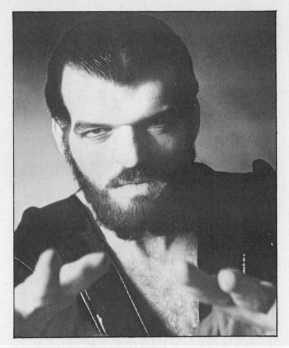

"Non is like a child," explains Jack O'Halloran. "He is not as cruel as the others. And he doesn't have the brains of an adult. He gets a real kick out of his powers. They are like a game to him."

O'Halloran knows about games. He was a football player for the Philadelphia Eagles. In 1966, he gave up football and became a heavyweight boxer. He won 60 fights. Then the doctors told him to give up boxing. He decided to try acting.

After seeing him play Non, audiences everywhere agree that O'Halloran is still a heavyweight!

INSIDE INFO SECTION!

Amaze your friends with these facts they probably don't know!

• Before he won the role of Superman, the most money Christopher Reeve ever earned was $150 a week.

• Robert Redford, Clint Eastwood, and James Caan were offered the part of Superman. All three turned it down. Redford wanted too much money. Eastwood said he was too busy. And Caan said there was no way he'd get into that "silly suit."

• Superman (Christopher Reeve) and Mork (Robin Williams) are close friends. They studied acting together at a school in New York City. They even appeared together on a stage once. They were on TV's *Saturday Night Live*—for five seconds.

• Superman, as played by Christopher Reeve, has a lot of powers the original Superman didn't have. He can stand up to the heat of the sun. He can fly faster than the speed of light. And he can fly across the universe. The early Superman's powers were not as great. In the *Superman* comics, Superman could leap only one-eighth of a mile; hurdle a 20-story building; raise tremendous weights; run faster than an express train; and nothing less than a bursting shell could break through his skin.

• For a short time, Clark Kent and Lois Lane were married. This happened only in the *Superman* newspaper comic strip. Then after a while, the writer decided it wasn't a good idea. He changed it by saying it was all a dream. It had never really happened.

• Superman, according to the comic books, will not live forever. Though we cannot see him growing older, someday he will get old and die.

• Margot Kidder says that it took Christopher Reeve more than 50 tries before he was able to leap off her balcony correctly. Reeve celebrated his 25th birthday during the filming of *Superman I*. Everyone there joked that they hoped he'd get his flying right before it was time to apply for Medicare!

• Here's a scene that was filmed but never used: In this scene, Lois Lane jumps out a window of the *Daily Planet* building. "I jump because I think Clark Kent is Superman," said Margot Kidder. "I want to see if he will reveal his true identity by rescuing me in midair." But Lois doesn't prove a thing. Superman breaks her fall with an awning. They spent a lot of time filming this scene, but then they decided not to use it. That's show business!

These pre-production sketches show a rescue by Superman. The school bus teeters and is

about to fall, but Superman lifts it up and sets it back on the bridge. Note that each camera angle is sketched out exactly, as is the position of each person in the scene. Hundreds of sketches were done for each film.

A fabulous
photo collection
of

SUPERMAN
MEMORIES
AND MAGIC!

The origin of Superman has appeared several times over the years. Here is the first portrayal as it appeared in 1939.

As the lad grew older, he learned to his delight that he could hurdle skyscrapers . . .

... LEAP AN EIGHTH OF A MILE ...

... RAISE TREMENDOUS WEIGHTS ...

... RUN FASTER THAN A STREAMLINE TRAIN —

...AND NOTHING LESS THAN A BURSTING SHELL COULD PENETRATE HIS SKIN!

WHAT TH' — ? THIS IS THE SIXTH HYPODERMIC NEEDLE I'VE BROKEN ON YOUR SKIN!

TRY AGAIN, DOC!

THE PASSING AWAY OF HIS FOSTER-PARENTS GREATLY GRIEVED CLARK KENT. BUT IT STRENGTHENED A DETERMINATION THAT HAD BEEN GROWING IN HIS MIND.

CLARK DECIDED HE MUST TURN HIS TITANIC STRENGTH INTO CHANNELS THAT WOULD BENEFIT MANKIND · AND SO WAS CREATED--

SUPERMAN

CHAMPION OF THE OPPRESSED, THE PHYSICAL MARVEL WHO HAD SWORN TO DEVOTE HIS EXISTENCE TO HELPING THOSE IN NEED!

The Great SUPERMAN III Mini-Magazine

by Chip Lovitt

Design and Layout by Margo Hrubec

The Ultimate Battle Between
MAN AND MACHINE

You can't keep a good man down, especially if the man happens to be Superman. The mighty Man of Steel, once again played by actor Christopher Reeve, has returned to the screen in a new adventure: *Superman III*. In this movie, the man from the planet Krypton meets a thoroughly modern menace and the perfect villain of the 1980s—the ultimate computer, as tall as a four-story building.

Along with the computer, Superman faces another unlikely enemy—the bumbling but ingenious Gus Gorman. Little did Gus realize when he saw the matchbook advertisement, "Make Big Money As a Computer Programmer," that it would eventually bring him face to face with Superman in a dramatic and deadly confrontation.

Gus and the megalomaniac millionaire, Ross Webster (played by Robert Vaughn), transform the mammoth computer from a useful tool into an awesome weapon with incredible powers. In the words of *Superman III* director Richard Lester, the machine becomes "a criminally insane computer, a silicon psychopath." This ultimate computer has the power to control the weather, alter the environment, and even create worldwide chaos. And as movie audiences find out, it also has the power to give Superman the fight of his life.

The Return of
THE GIRL NEXT DOOR

Superman's usual leading lady, Lois Lane, appears briefly in *Superman III*. But Lois plays second fiddle to a character new to the movies: Lana Lang. Comic book fans need no introduction to this red-haired heroine. In the comic book adventures of Superboy, Lana lived next door to the Kents. Lana often suspected that Clark Kent and Superboy were one and the same. Yet she could never prove it, and she could never really make herself believe that the meek and mousy Clark was actually the Boy of Steel in disguise. Clark always had a secret crush on Lana. But because he was always busy saving the world from disaster, he didn't have time for girl-friends.

Annette O'Toole is the actress who plays Lana in the movie. She summed up her character's relationship, past and present, with Clark: "When they were growing up in Smallville, Lana was into being popular. She thought Clark was a nerd. But now she's grown-up, and when she meets Clark again at the reunion, she's smitten."

Unlike Margot Kidder, who, as Lois Lane, got to fly with Superman in the two previous pictures, Annette keeps both feet on the ground in *Superman III*. "My one regret," Annette later recalled, "was not getting to fly with Superman in the movie. But Margot Kidder offered to lend me the 'rig' she used in the flying scenes, and Chris arranged with the technicians to take me up for a brief spin for fun. It was exhilarating."

Fantastic Facts About
SUPERMAN'S SUPER-POWERS

I n *Superman III*, audiences
get to see Superman use
many of his powers. With his
flying ability and super-strength,
he saves a crippled jet airliner.
His X-ray vision and super-hearing help him locate and save a
young boy lost in a huge field of
tall wheat. A blast of his super-
breath blows away a hurricane
and cleans up a huge oil spill.

But did you know that Superman's powers also include these
earthshaking abilities?

• His super-speed allows him to fly faster than the speed of light. In fact, he's fast enough to break the time barrier and travel both forward and backward in time!

• His heat vision can range from a warm ray, gentle enough to dry Clark Kent's wet clothes, to temperatures capable of melting steel. The first time Clark tried to use his heat vision when he was a teenager, his glasses melted. Now he has special lenses that can withstand the heat.

THIS IS A JOB FOR...

SUPERMAN

• By using his super-hearing, Superman can act as a one-man bomb squad, locating and then defusing ticking time bombs. By listening to someone's heartbeat and pulse, he can act as a human lie detector and determine whether or not someone is telling the truth.

• Superman's X-ray vision can see through anything, except lead. Superman didn't have X-ray vision in his early comic book adventures. If a criminal was hiding from Superman in a building, the only way the Man of Steel could spot him was to crash through the roof of the building. As one comic book editor pointed out, "The invention of X-ray vision proved to be a great roof-saver."

You Can GO HOME AGAIN

In *Superman III* Clark Kent returns to his hometown of Smallville. He has been assigned by *Daily Planet* editor Perry White to write a story on his high school class reunion. The trip is filled with memories of the days when Clark constantly had to play the timid teenager in order to protect his secret identity. To avoid suspicion, Clark pretended to be a second-

rate student and a flop on the football field.

Although the setting for Smallville in the movie appears to be a typical farming town in the United States, those scenes were actually filmed in High River, a small town in Alberta, Canada.

One scene set in Smallville was *really* hot stuff. The scene calls for Superman to put out a huge chemical factory fire that threatens to destroy the town. Using a combination of an icy blast of super-breath and his super-strength, Superman puts out the blaze and saves the town.

Superman's fire-fighting makes a spectacular scene, but it took a lot of work to set up. There was no big factory near High River, so the film crew had

to search for another location to stage the fire. They found the perfect place in the nearby city of Calgary, where several large oil refineries were located. But then the crew ran into trouble with the city officials. At first, the officials understandably did not want to give the movie company permission to start a huge fire there. Finally, however, the producers and crew were able to convince them that there would be no real disaster. They would take every precaution to keep the fire under control, they said, and to make sure, local firefighters and firefighting equipment were standing by. Luckily, everything went smoothly, and the scene was filmed without an accident. You might say that all the worrying was just a false alarm.

The Inside Story Behind

A SPECTACULAR SCENE

ost of the action in *Superman III* was filmed at Pinewood Studios in London, a place where movie magic is made every day. One of the scenes required more than the usual movie magic. It also required plenty of movie muscle.

The scene is a huge auto graveyard where Superman and Clark Kent become two separate persons. The two fight a bitter battle. In this sequence, special effects director Colin Chivers hoped to top the big fight scene between Superman and Zod in *Superman II.*

But the film company had a major problem. They needed dozens of junked American cars for the scene. Where in England could they find that many smashed-up American cars? The production designer Peter

Murton tells how the problem was solved: "We heard about this American in England whose business was finding spare parts for American vehicles." Murton called the man. The man said he did indeed have plenty of demolished Detroit-made cars, but that he was about to move them all to a new location. As luck would have it, the new site wasn't ready at the time. Murton saw a chance to make a deal.

"What if we take your cars off your hands for a few days," Murton asked. "Then we'll move them to your new location and we'll pay you for the privilege." So the film crew and a convoy of flatbed trucks hauled the wrecked cars to the studio lot at Pinewood. As you can see from the fight scene, the effort paid off nicely.

A Colorful KRYPTONITE CASEBOOK

No Superman story would be complete without the presence of Kryptonite, the only substance that can kill Superman. In *Superman III*, villains Ross Webster and Gus Gorman use their ultimate computer to get hold of some Kryptonite to use against Superman.

Kryptonite was formed out of the planet Krypton, the place where Superman was born. When the planet exploded, the blast sent billions of bits of rock hurtling through space. As the pieces of the planet passed through radioactive clouds and cosmic dust, they were transformed into a strange, new element called Kryptonite.

Only two types of Kryptonite are mentioned in the movie—green and red. But in Superman comics, there has been a variety of colorful types of Kryptonite. Green, of course, is the most powerful and most abundant kind. It can kill Superman. Only lead can stop the deadly rays of green Kryptonite.

Red Kryptonite has a weird effect on Superman—there's no telling what it will do. Superman was once exposed to red Kryptonite as he battled giant ants from space. It got him really bugged—he actually grew a huge ant head. Luckily for Superman, the effects of red Kryptonite are only temporary.

In the pre-production painting for *Superman II*, an artist imagined what Superman and Lois would look like flying over the bright lights of Metropolis at night. The actual filmed version captured the same magic of romance and free flight.

FLASHBACK!

The story behind the SUPERMAN LEGEND

It was a hot summer night in Cleveland, Ohio, in the year 1933. It was one of the worst years of The Great Depression. The song most often played on the radio was "Brother, Can You Spare a Dime?"

Jerry Siegel was a high school student in Cleveland. Jerry liked to read comic books and adventure magazines. *Dick Tracy, Flash Gordon, Buck Rogers*— Jerry read them all. And he wrote reviews of these comics for his school newspaper.

On that summer night, Jerry put his comic books aside and went to bed. He tossed and turned. He couldn't sleep. Scenes of the adventures he had been reading rushed through his mind.

Suddenly, Jerry had an idea. "All of a sudden, it hit me," he remembered later. "I thought of a character like Samson, Hercules, and all the strong men I ever heard of rolled into one. Only more so."

Much more so.

Jerry was so excited over his idea, he couldn't sleep. Early the next morning, he ran over to see his friend, Joe Shuster. Joe was a cartoonist. He quickly got just as excited as Jerry about the idea

Kirk Alyn appeared as Superman in two movie serials of the late 1940's. Those baggy tights wouldn't do today!

of a new kind of hero.

Joe began drawing sketch after sketch. Soon the two high school students began writing and drawing their hero's first adventure.

Superman was born.

Well . . . not quite. It took another six years for the young men to sell the idea to a comic book publisher!

Joe and Jerry graduated from high school. Then they went to work for DC Comics. They created a character named Slam Bradley and worked on

that for a while. Finally, in 1938, DC Comics decided to take a chance with Superman.

Action Comics #1 came out in June of 1938. It had Superman on the cover. The story inside was really written for a newspaper comic strip. It began in the middle of an action scene. Later, Jerry wrote some new pages to lead up to that scene. The whole story then appeared in a new comic book, *Superman #1*.

Today, most people think the story in *Action #1* left out the beginning by mistake!

But mistake or not, nothing could keep Superman from taking off. The comic book quickly sold out and more had to be printed. Soon Superman had a comic book of his own.

(*Action Comics #1* sold for a dime in 1938. Recently, someone paid more than $10,000 for a copy of it!)

MARY? SARAH? JONATHAN? EBEN?

The way Siegel and Shuster drew Superman in his early adventures is pretty much the way he still appears. But as the comic book got more popular, several changes were made.

At first, Superman's foster parents on Earth were named John and Mary Kent. Their names were later changed to Eben and Sarah Kent. It was explained that Clark was Sarah's maiden name. But the comic book stories of the early 1950's decided forever on Jonathan and Martha, which are the names used in the newest movies.

The name of Clark Kent's newspaper also changed. In one issue, it was called *The Daily Star*. In the next, the name changed. The newspaper was called *The Daily Planet*. Soon after, its editor, George Taylor, had his name changed to Perry White! For some reason the *Superman* radio show had decided to change the names of the paper and the editor, so the comic books changed, too.

Even the evil Lex Luthor went through changes. At first he had red hair. Today, as we all know, Luthor can comb his hair with a wash rag! (He's bald!)

Other heroes soon sprung to life in comics. Such characters as Blue Bolt, Catman, Doll Man, Blue Beetle, White Streak, and Neon the Unknown tried to be like Superman. But Superman was so popular that comic books alone weren't big enough to hold his adventures.

"THIS IS A JOB FOR . . ."

The *Superman* radio show began in 1940. As a 15-minute show every weekday, *Superman* had a huge audience. Each day,

George Reeves brought Superman to television. The series from the 1950's is still seen in many cities.

Trouble for Clark Kent in this early strip from 1938.

the program began with these words:

Faster than a speeding bullet!

More powerful than a locomotive!

Able to leap tall buildings at a single bound!

Look! Up in the sky!

It's a bird!

It's a plane!

IT'S SUPERMAN!

A young radio actor named Bud Collyer played both Clark Kent and Superman on the show. When he wanted the radio audience to know he was changing from Clark to Super-

man, he would make his voice sound really low and say:

This is a job

for

SUPERMAN!

People just couldn't get enough of the Man of Steel. In the 1940's, a movie company made several color cartoons about him. Then another company decided to do a movie serial about Superman. They hired an actor named Kirk Alyn to play the part.

In 1951, an actor named George Reeves took over the part. Reeves had been an actor in Hollywood for many years. He had even had a part in the famous movie, *Gone with the Wind.*

George Reeves brought Superman to TV. The Superman

show was on for seven years. It had a low budget, and the same flying scenes were used over and over again. But TV watchers loved it. The show is still being seen on many TV stations today —even though it was made nearly 30 years ago.

Sometimes, being TV's Superman was a hard job for George Reeves. One day at a shopping center, a boy tried to shoot him with a real gun. The boy thought Reeves really was Superman, so he thought the bullets would bounce off him.

After that, Reeves never appeared in public in his Superman costume.

"THE MAN OF TOMORROW TODAY"

A few things have changed about the comic book Superman in recent years. Clark Kent now spends part of his time at *The Daily Planet* and part at WGBS-TV where he is a newsman. His TV boss is Morgan Edge. Instead of green Kryptonite, Superman now has to worry about many colors of Kryptonite!

Meanwhile, on the big movie screen, Christopher Reeve is

Clark is assigned to cover himself in these panels from the late 1930's.

proving that man can really fly. And he is proving that the Superman legend—which started more than 40 years ago— may be just beginning!

BEHIND-THE-CAMERAS SECRETS

We answer your questions about the making of THE SUPERMAN MOVIES!

Q How did Superman fly? Was it all done with trick photography?

A The flying in the *Superman* movies wasn't all trick photography—but it *was* tricky. For most flying scenes, Christopher Reeve was hanging from wires. The wires were painted so you couldn't see them. They were hung from a crane that could raise Reeve up and down.

In one scene, the crane held him 240 feet above the East River in New York City. But most of the time he was only about 30 to 40 feet off the ground. (Reeve did all of his own flying.)

For close-up shots, no wires were needed. Reeve simply leaned forward into a wind made by a giant fan. To make it look as if he was flying with the birds, crew members threw birds past him!

Q Is it true that Christopher Reeve had hundreds of Superman costumes? Is it true that he never wore the same one twice?

A Not exactly. Several different Superman suits were made for him. Each had a different use. Some suits were made to look great while Superman was standing. Others were made for sitting, leaping, flying, or coming in for a landing. The flying cape had hidden wires under it. The wires made the cape billow even when there was no wind.

In *Superman II*, Reeve went through 40 different suits. As soon as one would get snagged or sweaty, he'd change it. He didn't want anyone to see Superman with wrinkled tights!

Sketch shows Superman costume as designed by Yvonne Blake, who designed all costumes for the movies.

Q Does Christopher Reeve really have all those muscles? Or did he use padding to make himself look stronger?

A When he was picked for the part, Reeve was way too thin to fill out Superman's costume. "Most of my exercise up to that point had been mental," he admits. The producers wanted to give him padding to make his muscles look bigger. But Reeve didn't like the idea.

"I just couldn't face the thought of playing the part with fake muscles," he says. "I had to get into shape so that I could believe that I was Superman!"

David Prowse was called in to help. Prowse should be known to most movie fans. He played Darth Vader in the *Star Wars* films. He trained Reeve, and he was tough!

In the morning, Reeve ran. Then he lifted weights for two hours. Then Reeve spent 90 minutes on a trampoline. All the while, he ate four high-protein meals a day.

"After the first workout, I went into the locker room and was sick," Reeve admits. "But I kept at it."

All in all, he added about 30 pounds of muscle. Says Reeve: "I found muscles I never knew I had!"

Q Was the Eiffel Tower scene in *Superman II* really filmed at the Eiffel Tower?

A Yes. A lot of that exciting scene was really filmed in Paris, France, at the Eiffel Tower. But, of course, the moviemakers couldn't destroy any parts of the famous tower.

Instead, models of the tower were used. It took seven months to build several models. The models looked just like the real tower. That's because the designer used the original blueprints that were used to build the real Eiffel Tower!

Q Was the exciting battle between Superman and his three foes really filmed on the streets of New York? If so, how did they keep people from getting hurt?

A They kept people from getting hurt by *not* filming that big battle in New York. The entire fight took place on a set at a movie studio. It was one of the largest sets in movie history!

The set was made to look just like New York City's 42nd Street between Second and Third Avenues. It cost more than two million dollars to build!

The set had 30 lamp posts, 12 blinking traffic lights, 12 fire hydrants, three phone booths, and 50 neon signs. And it had enough cars, buses, and trucks to cause a giant traffic jam in any city in the world!

All of this was destroyed during the big battle with the villains.

THE LOWDOWN on LEX LUTHOR

THIS TIME I'M GOING TO GET RID OF MY NEMESIS ONCE AND FOR ALL...I'M GOING TO DESTROY SUPERMAN!

Why does Lex Luthor hate Superman so much? Well, the movies have one answer. But to get the whole answer, we have to go back to the early comic book days. Here is the *real* story. . . .

In the comics, the story begins when Lex Luthor saved Superboy's life. One day many years ago, Superboy was in his hometown of Smallville. He saw young Lex Luthor working on the Luthor family farm. Superboy flew over to meet him.

Suddenly, a meteorite made of Kryptonite landed. Lex Luthor pushed the meteorite over a cliff. That saved Superboy's life.

"Superboy, I'm your biggest fan," Luthor said. "Please come back to my house. I want to show you my Superboy scrapbooks."

Superboy wanted to repay Luthor. So he built him a science lab. He knew that one day Luthor would be a brilliant scientist. Luthor started to do experiments in his lab. He decided to find a cure for Kryptonite.

Then disaster struck.

Lex Luthor discovered a cure for Kryptonite. But a fire broke

out in his lab. Superboy was nearby. He flew to the fire. He put it out with a blast of his super-breath. But the blast of wind destroyed Luthor's projects. And the gas fumes from the fire caused all of his hair to fall out.

Lex Luthor thought Superboy did it on purpose. "You are jeal-ous of me!" he screamed at Superboy. "You wrecked my projects on purpose! You don't want me to become famous!"

So Lex Luthor destroyed the cure for Kryptonite. From that day on, he has been Superman's worst enemy! Says Lex Luthor: "There isn't room enough on Earth for Superman and me!"

Take the TRICKY SUPERMAN QUIZ!

When it comes to knowing all about the *Superman* movies, are you a hero? See how many of these hard questions you can answer. Circle the answer you think is right for each question. Then turn the page over. The right answers are written upside down at the end of the test. Good luck!

1 Marlon Brando plays Superman's father Jor-El. Susannah York plays Lara, his mother. What is the name of the young baby they send to Earth, who later becomes known as Superman?

a) Superbaby.
b) Jor-El, Jr.
c) Kal-El.
d) Lois Lane.

2 In *Superman I*, Superboy races past a train, and a female passenger looks out the window at him. Who was that passenger?

a) Christopher Reeve's mother.

b) Noel Neill, who played Lois Lane on the *Superman* TV series.

c) Miss Piggy.

d) Susannah York, who also played Lara, Jor-El's wife.

3 Gene Hackman gets his name in big letters at the beginning of *Superman*. In one famous comedy film his name wasn't mentioned at all—even though he gave one of the funniest performances of his career. That movie was called:

a) *King Kong.*

b) *Return from Witch Mountain.*

c) *Young Frankenstein.*

d) *Zorro.*

4 In *Superman I*, the underground hideout of Lex Luthor was actually designed to look like:

a) the San Diego Zoo.

b) the Empire State Building.

c) Yankee Stadium.

d) Grand Central Station.

5 What member of the cast of both *Superman* movies was a famous child star who started out in silent "Our Gang" comedies?

a) Margot Kidder.

b) Jackie Cooper.

c) Gene Hackman.

d) Christopher Reeve.

6 General Zod and his followers leave the moon and land in a small farm town in the United States. What is the name of that town?

a) East Houston, Idaho.

b) Des Moines, Iowa.

c) Pocatello, Idaho.

d) Smallville, Kansas.

7 Lex Luthor offers to help General Zod, Ursa, and Non. What does he ask for in return for his help?

a) He wants the right to kill Superman himself.

b) He wants to be named King of Australia.

c) He wants his life to be spared.

d) He wants to take over Superman's Fortress in the Arctic.

8 Lex Luthor always calls her Miss Teschmacher. But what is Miss Teschmacher's first name?

a) Margot.

b) Mary.

c) Eve.

d) Susannah.

9 John Williams has written music for many movies. He composed the music for *Superman*. For which of the following films did he NOT write the music?

a) *Jaws*.

b) *Star Wars*.

c) *The Empire Strikes Back*.

d) *Close Encounters of the Third Kind*.

ANSWERS

1. The son of Lara and Jor-El is named Kal-El (c).

2. Noel Neill was the passenger on the train. She was playing Lois Lane's mother (b).

3. Gene Hackman made a wacky appearance in *Young Frankenstein*. He played the blind man who poured hot soup on the monster (c).

4. Lex Luthor's lair looked a lot like New York City's famous Grand Central Station (d).

5. Jackie Cooper was a famous film star as a child. After the "Our Gang" comedies, he starred in the first version of *The Champ* (b).

6. They landed in East Houston, Idaho (a).

7. Lex Luthor wants to be named King of Australia. He doesn't get his wish (b).

8. Miss Teschmacher's first name is Eve (c).

9. A trick question. John Williams composed the music for all of these films. Gotcha! Or did we?